Improvising Bass Guitar

Intermediate Level

Written by
Tony Skinner

on behalf of
The Registry of Guitar Tutors

ISBN: 1-898466-32-7

A CIP record for this publication is available from the British Library.

© 1998 & 2004 Registry Publications

Published in Great Britain by

Registry Mews, 11 to 13 Wilton Road, Bexhill, Sussex, TN40 1HY

Typesetting by Take Note Publishing Ltd., Lingfield, Surrey

Printed in Great Britain

For information on bass guitar exams contact

Registry RGT
Registry of Guitar Tutors

Tel: 01424 22 22 22
www.RegistryOfGuitarTutors.com

Contents

CD running order

Track 1	Tuning guide	Track 8	R 'n' B
Track 2	'60s Soul	Track 9	Funky Rock
Track 3	Romantic Ballad	Track 10	Melodic Pop
Track 4	Moderate Rock	Track 11	Blues Rock
Track 5	Pop Rock	Track 12	Swing
Track 6	Jazzy Pop	Track 13	Modern Jazz
Track 7	Country Blues		

Introduction

The purpose of this book is to encourage bass players to improve their skills in improvisation, so that they can become confident and fluent in creating their own bass lines in a wide range of musical styles. For any bassist playing in, or wishing to join, a band this is an essential skill. However, the ability to improvise over chord sequences is often difficult to acquire unless you have someone on-hand to play the backing chords for you. Fortunately, the accompanying CD provides a full band backing track (minus the bass part) for all the musical examples shown within this book. By playing along with the CD you'll be able to hear how your bass lines sound in a real band setting. Use the tuning guide [CD TRACK 1] to make sure that you're fully in tune before you begin.

Bass Exams

This book is structured in line with the Registry Of Guitar Tutors bass guitar examination syllabus. It introduces the concept of improvisation at post-beginner level (Grade Three) and steadily progresses in a carefully structured way up to Grade Five level.

The book provides an ideal study aid for those preparing to take a bass guitar examination, however it is designed to be used by all bass players who wish to improve their improvisation skills - whether intending to take an examination or not.

Essential basics

Right hand

1. Alternate fingers

Pick the strings by alternating between your first and second fingers (known as index and middle) - never pick the same string repeatedly with the same finger; always alternate your picking. If using a plectrum, rather than fingers, to pick the strings, make sure that you alternate between downstrokes and upstrokes.

2. Use rest strokes

To get a strong tone and maintain control over your picking you need to use rest strokes. First rest the tip of your finger on the string you wish to play. The finger should then press toward, and finally come to rest on, the adjacent lower string. Avoid any temptation to pluck out from the guitar body.

Left hand

1. Use fingertips

Fret notes by pressing with the very tips of your fingers. As fingertips are less fleshy than the pads of the fingers it's much easier to fret notes with clarity and without the need to use excess pressure.

2. Aim for the edge

It's essential that you press at the very edge of the frets - right next to the fretwire. This minimises both buzzes and the amount of pressure required; enabling you to play with a lighter, clearer and more fluent touch.

Guitarographs

Throughout this book all musical information is illustrated using the Registry Of Guitar Tutors' unique Guitarograph system.

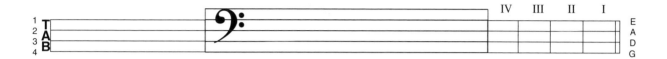

The *Guitarograph* uses a combination of tablature, traditional notation and fingerboard diagram. These are explained individually below:

(1) Tablature

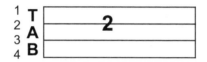

The horizontal lines represent the strings in descending order, as indicated. The numbers on the string lines refer to the frets at which the left-hand fingers should press. The above example therefore means: play on string 2 at fret 2.

(2) Bass clef notation

The lines and spaces of the bass clef indicate notes as follows:

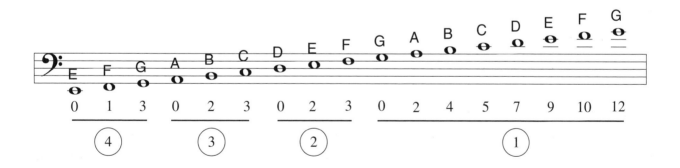

A sharp (#) before a note *raises* its pitch by a semitone, i.e. the note is played one fret higher.

A flat (♭) before a note *lowers* its pitch by a semitone, i.e. the note is played one fret lower.

In the above example, the circled numbers at the bottom refer to a string on which each note could be played. The other numbers refer to the fret on that string at which the note is to be found. The same note could be played on another string – so it is important to always refer to either the tablature or fingerboard diagram.

(3) Fingerboard diagram

Each horizontal line represents a string. The vertical lines represent the frets. Each fret is given a number in Roman numerals. Numbers on the horizontal lines indicate the left-hand finger to be used.

IV   III   II   I

Play at the 3rd fret of the D string using the 3rd finger.

Guitarograph

All three previous methods are ways of illustrating the same information. In this book all are used in combination, using the *guitarograph*. This leaves no doubt as to what is required.

This example therefore means: play string 3 at fret 3 (tablature),
play the note C (notation),
use finger 3 (fingerboard diagram).

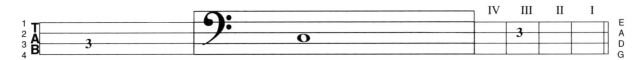

Above each *guitarograph* is an interval *formula*. This lists the letter names of the notes to be played, together with their *interval numbers*. The interval numbers refer to the position of the notes in comparison to the major scale of the same root. For example:

C Major Scale

note names:	C	D	E	F	G	A	B	C
interval number:	R	2	3	4	5	6	7	R

C Major Arpeggio

note names:	C		E		G			C
interval number:	R		3		5			R

Alternative positions and fingerings

When using the *guitarograph*, please remember that the *note names* given are definitive, that is, they cannot be changed. However, on the bass guitar, it is possible to play a note at more than one position on the fingerboard. For example, the note C given in the previous examples can also be played at the same pitch on string 4 at fret 8. This is called an alternative *position*.

It is also possible to play the arpeggios with fingers other than those indicated. There are various reasons why other fingers might be chosen. For example, on the bass guitar a major consideration is the size of a players hands, and the ability to stretch over several frets. The fingering given in this book, although carefully chosen as being generally suitable, is only one possible recommended suggestion. Feel free to use any alternative systematic fingering, provided that this produces a good musical result.

Grade Three

In order to create your own bass lines it is important that you have a thorough practical knowledge of arpeggios of all the common chords in all keys. A list of the most common chord types (and their abbreviations) is shown below.

major	(A)
minor	(Am)
major 7th	(AMaj7)
minor 7th	(Am7)
dominant 7th	(A7)

Examples of all these arpeggios are shown below starting on G and C - showing the patterns starting on the E string and the A string respectively. For other pitches refer to the table below which details the starting string and fret for each arpeggio in all 12 keys.

arpeggio	F♯/G♭	G	G♯/A♭	A	A♯/B♭	B	C	C♯/D♭	D	D♯/E♭	E	F
starting string	E	E	E	E	E	E	A	A	A	A	A	A
starting fret	2	3	4	5	6	7	3	4	5	6	7	8

G Major

G	B	D	G
R	3	5	R

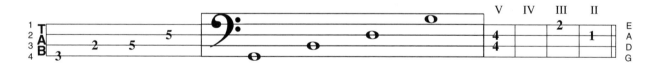

C Major

C	E	G	C
R	3	5	R

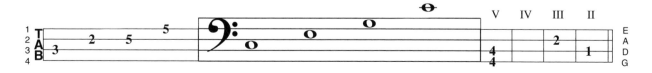

G Minor

```
G   Bb   D   G
R   b3   5   R
```

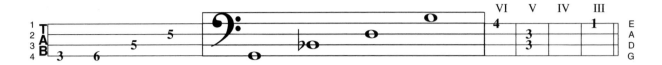

C Minor

```
C   Eb   G   C
R   b3   5   R
```

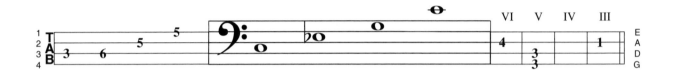

G Major 7

```
G   B   D   F#   G
R   3   5   7    R
```

C Major 7

```
C   E   G   B   C
R   3   5   7   R
```

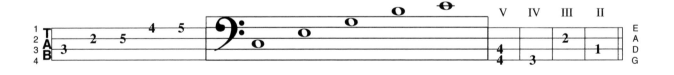

8

G Minor 7

G	B♭	D	F	G
R	♭3	5	♭7	R

C Minor 7

C	E♭	G	B♭	C
R	♭3	5	♭7	R

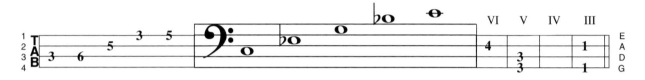

G Dominant 7

G	B	D	F	G
R	3	5	♭7	R

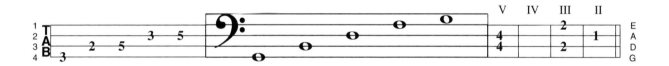

C Dominant 7

C	E	G	B♭	C
R	3	5	♭7	R

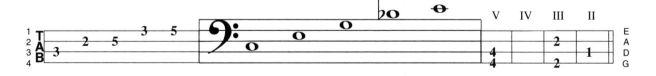

Getting started

Using the CD, play along with the chord progressions below. Start by listening to one verse of the sequence before you begin so that you can grasp the style, mood and tempo of the music. Listen carefully to hear when the chord changes occur. Begin to improvise by playing just the root note over each chord. Although you are only using one note within each bar you have total freedom over how many times you play that note within each bar - in other words you can create a rhythmic figure using that one note. The rhythm can be as simple or as creative as you like; as long as it suits the musical style of the track. At first, it's safest to maintain the same rhythm on all chords; you can experiment with variations once you are able to play through the sequence securely.

Root and fifth

Once you are able to play through all the sequences using root notes you can start to expand your range of improvisation by adding the fifth note of each chord. The fifth note can always be found two frets higher than the root note on the adjacent higher string. For notes on the A string, the fifth of the chord can also be played in a lower octave on the same fret as the root note, but on the adjacent lower string.

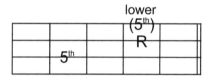

Using the CD, play along with the chord progressions again. This time experiment by occasionally adding a fifth note. At first you might like to establish a fixed bass pattern and alternate between the root and fifth in a regular way. Once you become used to incorporating the fifth note try and improvise a little more freely and vary the way that you use the fifth on different chords. There is no need to play the fifth on every chord; as long as you play the root note you will always stay in tune. How much use you make of the fifth note is really a matter of taste and style. As an improviser it's one of the decisions that you need to make based on your interpretation of the mood and tempo of the music.

Root, third and fifth

By adding the third note of a chord to your improvisations you will be able to make your bass lines much more melodic. Play along with the chord progressions again, this time experimenting by occasionally adding a third note to your improvisation. At first, try and establish a fixed bass pattern that uses the root, third and fifth in a regular way. But do remember that whereas the root and fifth notes are the same whether the chord is major or minor, the third note varies depending upon whether the chord is major or minor. Once you become used to incorporating the third note, try and improvise a little more freely and vary the way that you use the third on different chords. There is no need to play the third on every chord - how much use you make of the third note is really a matter of taste and what you think best suits the musical style. Listen carefully to the backing track in order to choose an appropriate style of bass line.

Octave and seventh

Notice that each arpeggio includes the root note twice. Once low (at the beginning of the arpeggio) and once high (at the end of the arpeggio). The high root note is known as the octave. This is a very useful note to include in your bass lines as it adds range and a sense of movement, and because it is simply the root note (but higher) it will always be in tune no matter what the type of chord.

The final step at this level is to try occasionally adding a seventh note to your improvisation. This will help you bring out the distinctive harmony of the seventh chords. Do bear in mind that there is no need to play the seventh note on every seventh chord. Attempting to use the root, third, fifth, seventh and octave over each chord would undoubtedly make your bass line sound too busy and over fussy. Sometimes the saying 'less is more' gives the best clue to establishing the right 'feel' for a piece of music. Before you begin to play, listen carefully to at least one verse of the backing track in order to choose an appropriate style of bass line.

Backing tracks

CD TRACK 2 – '60s Soul

$\left|\dfrac{4}{4}\right.$ A♭ | Fm | Cm7 | Cm7 | A♭ | Fm | D♭ | E♭7 ‖

CD TRACK 3 – Romantic Ballad

$\left|\dfrac{3}{4}\right.$ E♭Maj7 | Fm | Cm | B♭ | E♭Maj7 | Gm | Fm | B♭7 ‖

CD TRACK 4 – Moderate Rock

$\left|\dfrac{6}{8}\right.$ F♯m | E | D | E | F♯m | E | Bm7 | C♯m7 ‖

CD TRACK 5 – Pop Rock

$\left|\dfrac{4}{4}\right.$ E | EMaj7 | A | AMaj7 | F♯m7 | G♯m7 | A | B7 ‖

Grade Four

At this stage it best to remain concentrating on improvising over the most commonly occurring chords. A list of these (and their abbreviations) is shown below.

major	(C)
minor	(Cm)
major 7th	(CMaj7)
minor 7th	(Cm7)
dominant 7th	(C7)

At this level you should start to become familiar with the arpeggios for each chord in TWO different fingerboard positions. This will allow you much more flexibility and freedom of movement in your playing. Examples of each arpeggio type are shown below with a root note of C. These shapes are moveable to other keys. If you are unfamiliar with the single fingerboard shapes for any of these arpeggios you should thoroughly revise the Grade Three chapter within this book before proceeding.

C Major

C	E	G	C
R	3	5	R

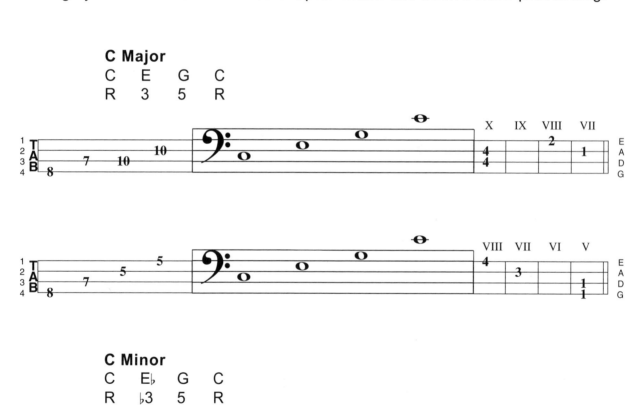

C Minor

C	E♭	G	C
R	♭3	5	R

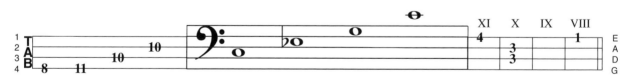

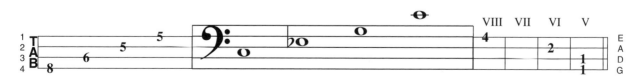

C Major 7

C	E	G	B	C
R	3	5	7	R

C Minor 7

C	E♭	G	B♭	C
R	♭3	5	♭7	R

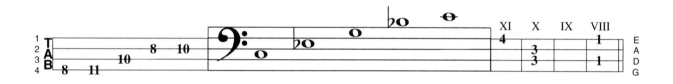

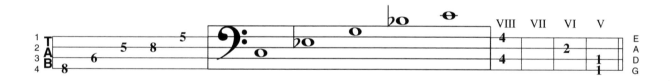

C Dominant 7

C	E	G	B♭	C
R	3	5	♭7	R

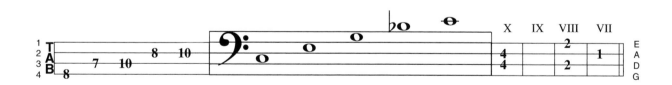

Playing with the backing tracks

Before you begin to play, listen carefully to at least one verse of the backing track in order to choose an appropriate style of bass line. Remember, there is no need to use the root, third, fifth, seventh and octave repeatedly over each chord. This would undoubtedly make your bass line sound too busy and over fussy. How much use you make of notes other than the root is really a matter of taste and style. As an improviser, it's one of the decisions that you need to make based on your interpretation of the mood and tempo of the music. Always be aware that just because all the notes from an arpeggio will be in tune with a particular chord this does not mean that playing all of these notes will result in the best musical effect. Use the arpeggios as a framework to help you maintain accuracy and as an aid to bring out the harmony of the chords, but do not neglect the importance of developing a musical 'feel' and 'groove'. Fortunately, by having access to the accompanying CD you will be able to get plenty of practice in playing along with a band in a variety of musical styles.

Backing tracks

CD TRACK 6 – Jazzy Pop

| $\frac{3}{4}$ B♭ | B♭Maj7 | E♭Maj7 | E♭Maj7 | Dm7 | Dm7 | Gm7 | F7 |

CD TRACK 7 – Country Blues

| $\frac{6}{8}$ B | G♯m7 | G♯m7 | F♯ | B | D♯m7 | D♯m7 | EMaj7 |

CD TRACK 8 – R 'n' B

| $\frac{4}{4}$ A♭7 D♭7 | A♭7 E♭7 | D♭7 | A♭7 | D♭7 | E♭7 |

CD TRACK 9 – Funky Rock

| $\frac{4}{4}$ C♯m7 | F♯m7 | B | C♯m7 | AMaj7 | AMaj7 | B | G♯7 |

14

Grade Five

At this stage you should have a good practical knowledge of arpeggios in two fingerboard positions for all basic major, minor and seventh chords. If you lack knowledge or fluency in this area it is strongly recommended that you thoroughly revise the preceding chapters of this book before proceeding. In all cases, you are advised to read through the text of the preceding chapters as they contain important advice on how to approach improvisation.

By this level you should start to gain some knowledge of a few other chord types such as minor and major 6ths and suspended 4ths. These chords are quite widely used in many styles of popular music. They are illustrated below in two different fingerboard positions - each with a root note of C. The shapes are moveable to other pitches.

C Sus 4

C	F	G	C
R	4	5	R

C Major 6

C	E	G	A	C
R	3	5	6	R

15

C Minor 6

C	E♭	G	A	C
R	♭3	5	6	R

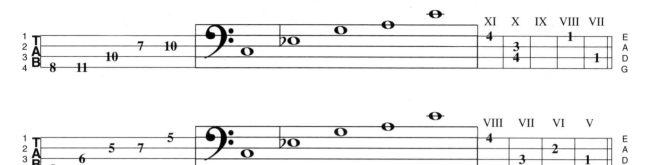

Playing along with the backing tracks

Before you begin to improvise your own bass lines over the backing tracks it is recommended that you read through the paragraph in the Grade Four chapter entitled 'playing along with the backing tracks'. If you haven't already done so, reading through the text of the Grade Three chapter would also prove helpful.

CD TRACK 10 – Melodic Pop

| 3/4 GMaj7 | Am6 | C6 | Dsus4 | Bm | Em7 | Dsus4 | D ‖ |

CD TRACK 11 – Blues Rock

| 6/8 Fm7 | D♭ | E♭ | C7 | Fm7 | B♭m7 | C7 | C7 ‖ |

CD TRACK 12 – Swing

| 4/4 C6 | Am7 | C6 | Am7 | Dm6 | Dm6 | Em7. A7. | Dm7. G7. ‖ |

CD TRACK 13 – Modern Jazz

| 4/4 Bm6 | F♯7 | Bm6 | F♯7 | Em | Em7 | A6 | F♯7 ‖ |